# Breathe Under
# The
# Moon

# SHINee World
# ( Shawols )

" The pretty words you left

behind, became a poem"

Published by
**T G I B T   P r e s s**
An Imprint of "**The Great Indian Book Tour**"
www.tgibt.com
106/91, Ashok marg, Vijay path
Mansarover, Jaipur, Rajasthan-302020
Phone : +91-72400-68114
email : prashant@tgibt.com

Title    : Breathe Under the Moon
Editor  : Suhani Hanotwal
Copyright © Suhani Hanotwal 2021
All rights reserved

First published in 2021
First Edition 2021

# Contents

# COMPILER'S NOTE

There is no shortcut to perfection,
All it takes is hard-work and
More hard-work.
**~SHINee's JongHyun**

It took me a lot of efforts to fulfil my dream,
to write a book dedicated to JongHyun.
And it is aptly said that
*"Dream and you can achieve your goals
anytime soon."*

And here we are, shawols from all around the
world are writing poems to express their
love and emotions for our
beloved Kpop idol Kim JongHyun.

Though all of us had our own works, still
each one of the writers contributing
worked really hard and fought
against all odds so that this book can be
published on JongHyun's birthday.

And I don't know how to thank them enough.
And that without them, I don't know if this

book will be there or not.
All I wanna conclude this note is by saying that
"Tho we see SHINee as 4 on stage but in our hearts, it will forever be 5."

And I wanna wish the writers, all the very best for their future and I hope they find all kinds of happiness, only happiness.


With love
**Suhani Hanotwal**

# Co-authors

Suhani Hanotwal (India)

Ratna Haryati (Indonesia)

Mohima Sarkar (India)

Majda Ulfat (Pakistan)

Yuva Karnika (India)

M.M. Kavindi Chathurya Munasinghe
(Sri Lanka)

Sofea (Malaysia)

Samprikta Das (India)

Noora Baloch (Bahrain)

Najia Essa Kashcool (Palestine)

Jennifer Thomas (India)

Shainy Prarthana (Sri Lanka)

B.K.D.Dinel (Dino) (Sri Lanka)

Jasia samreen (Pakistan)

P. Deekshitha (India)

Agamya Sharma (India)

Syna Kaur Anand (India)

Gayathri Chandrasiri (Sri Lanka )

# Poems for
# Kim Jonghyun

# Your Voice

When the world feels alien
When everything gets dark
When my days get long
And my lonely self feels stranded
When I lose my strength to continue
When everything crumbles to pieces
when my courage and hope crashes
When nothing works out
My burdened and wounded heart is
comforted
by your words, by your voice
When I hear your voice
I feel as If my heart is all healed
I feel as if I can start over once again
Even if walking in scorching sun thanks to
you I walk as
if I breathe under the moon

**~ Majda Ulfat**

# Lighting star in my life

I was in a beautiful room in others mind
But it was a dark cage for myself
I tried to find a way out,
I tried to find a reason to live

I shouted,
I screamed on pain,
I cried till my eyes became red
I tried to bite the Iron Gate
I tried to push the no-exist gate
But there was no hope left to me
I almost give up,
It was hard to explain someone
Finally I tried to accept my fate and try live
inside that dark cage
Tried to forget about the life outside of cage

But one day I saw a bling bling light comes to
me with a beautiful smile and kind words
His warm words burned the iron gate and
came

through it he made a gate that I couldn't make
even I tried
He gave me a hand by his comforting words
and shining eyes
Putting on his hands on my weak shoulders
Saying few words I was dying to hear from
someone
"You did well...
You are not a leftover
You tired your best
Show them what you got
You still have hope"

He walked away with big smile and told me to
follow his sweet voice
I walked through the Iron Gate by following
his warm words
So much encouragement
So much care
So much love
I never felt it
He covered my eyes in case if I get hurt
He opened my eyes when I got out

Finally I saw the world outside that I wanted to
see
I felt so cold but he gave me a blanket of his
warm words
I felt so warm and safe
Now I can see the world through him
I came a long journey with him

He still showing me light when I am
alone in dark
Smiling to me as a shining star
Joking with his funny talks
But I always regretting for something
I followed him for more than 13 years in my
life
I was failed to say something to him
Today I want to say it
YOU DID WELL More than anyone else. And
I love you so much
for making my life back to a bright life.
**I WILL BE ALWAYS WITH YOU
FOREVER!**

**~ Gayathri Chandasiri**

# ART

Every time I pick up a pen to write you a song
All I find is silence...
How do you put into words a decade, where
you gave me
balance?

There was nothing in me but defiance
You completed me, like the moon completes
our rhymes
And just like the moon you too heard me out,
never did you whine.

Would it not have been different? If I heard
you out in actions ?
Would it not have changed? If I put in efforts,
even just a fraction?
It's been three years and I still feel you
But as I hear your songs, I feel guilt too.

You stood by my side like a shield , without a
bias
Shouldn't I have shielded you too? When they
came at you
with malice.
"You did good, you did well", I chant it now
like a hymn
If I only said it enough then when the light in
your eyes kept
getting dim
I've learnt my lesson now, I pray I don't lose
anyone like I did
But honestly my dearest friend, I feel like I still
have you deep within my skin
So be happy where you are, shining like you
always did in my heart
For I will always remember you Kim JongHyun
as Poet| Artist
and Art.


~ Jennifer Thomas

# Magical Letter to Heaven

I am Sending a dove with a
Magical Letter
Inside are million kisses
With warm hugs
To say how much I
Miss you love you too
I miss your voice so much more
Don't stay in heaven too long
Come to earth and sing your song
We will hear it Thousand years
And more


~ M. M. Kavindi Chathurya
Munasinghe

# THANKFUL...

The words you left behind
Those heavenly smiles
Forever so bright
Shines our lives.


~ B. K. D.  Dinel ( Dino)

# Sunshine

Our sweet poet of night,
Your words are our shining light.
Your heart is so precious,
Your smile is our sunshine!


~ **Jasia Samreen**

# Thank you Note

My gratitude and love can never be expressed
in these verses of poetry
Absolutely no word is enough
I have so many thankyous to say
so many words to relay

Thank you for being my pride
Thank you for being by my side
Thank you for helping me overcome every tide
Thank you for not letting me runway or hide

Thank you for being my muse
Thank you for not letting me lose
Thank you for being my light in my blues
Thank you for confidence to break unjust
queues

I thank you for being you
for always being true
through and through
in everything you loved to do
~ **Majda Ulfat**

# Beautiful Melody

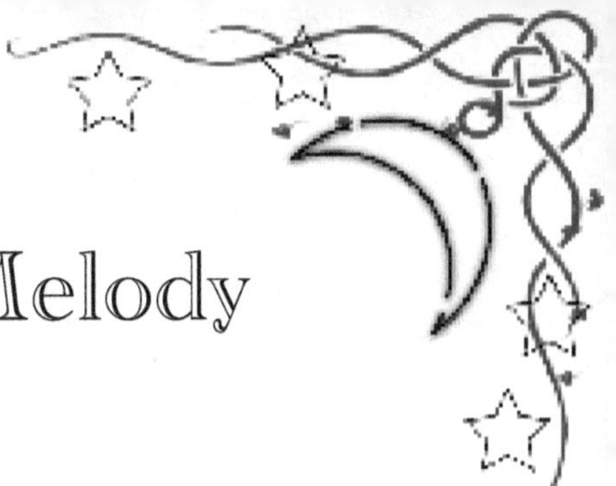

At the quite sleepless night
I looked at the stars
Shining lightly and brightly
Suddenly heard a beautiful
Melody with a
Sweet voice

A voice that I know
I adore
He is singing from Heaven
I closed my eyes and whispered
"I love you Jonghyun, you did well"


~ M. M. Kavindi Chathurya
Munasinghe

# The reason why I stand up again

I used to sing
I used to be more bright and cheerful person
But I had few critical failures in my life
I almost gave up my everything
I was hurt
One day Doctors said that I never can sing
again
I never can hit a high pitch
So I tried to spend my life as a loser
I gained weight because of stress
People who loved me because of my voice they
all left me

My second critical failure
I failed 2 times from my university entrance
exam
I wanted to hide from world
I was so embarrassed
I was angry myself

I wanted to kill myself
I hated myself for not been perfect
I heard so many scolding everyday
I locked myself inside 4 walls
Only my dogs were there to talk with

I was so lonely inside that dark hole
I heard angel voice saying you did well and
saying
put my shoulders on his arm
And let's end the hardest day together
Gave me hope
Gave me courage
Gave me strength to walk out proudly

His heart-felt words were honey to my ears
and drive me to work more hard and to show
what I have got
I tried to follow his steps one by one
Tired to sing again even doctors said I never
can do
I succeed

I was a terrible dancer
But I showed I can dance
I was scared to audience
But I danced in front of a big crowd
I sang his songs in front television
I am happy to make him proud
Oppa are you watching me over there?
Did I really do well?
You are my teacher who told me what I should
do


I faced my university entrance exams and got
All A Marks and got a high rank from country
and got into best college
He never told me directly but his sincere words
reminded me
who am I
What I can do
He showed me nothing is impossible


Oppa can you see me?
Are you proud of me?

I am a good student, right?
I always wanted to ask
Do you know what his answer was?
He blings his star so happily and replied to me
You did well and I am happy for you

Thank you for being my legs
Thank you for being my backbone
Thank you for being my backup
Thank you for born as Kim Jong Hyun
Thank you for making me perfect
Thank you for letting me who am i
Thank you for your music
Thank you for being my melody
Always love you and always with you my
strength


~ Gayathri Chandasiri

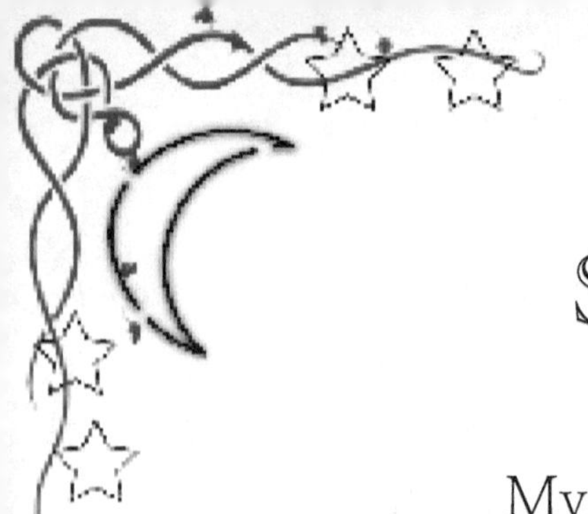

# SPARK

My morning starts,
with your smile on my mind.
And ends,
with a spark in my eyes.


# FOREVER

My love for you is like,
A constant flowing river.
Don't know when it started,
And where it will end.


**~ Suhani Hanotwal**

# Because, I am your prize

Take me in your arms,
Let's hug each other for one last time today.

I say I'm proud of you,
You hugged me softly.

Did you really hear my voice?
Maybe you did,
Atleast that's what I'd believe.

Even though you leave me alone all day,
You still wait to see me running to you while
wailing my tails.

I crawl into your big hoodies,
I know you feel home in my warmth.

You sang me stories and songs,
I'm playfully listening to you.
You laugh and cry, Till your eyes get dry.

I keep jumping around you as if there's no
tomorrow.

We eventually doze off,
The day still repeats like that one song on
loop
But I'm still amazed by you. ---


~ Yuva Karnika

# Everlasting Song

Even in the dust of time
if everything gets faded
one thing wont ever get old
it shall remain precious as gold
it will always be afresh and new
years won't matter whether many or a few
your memories
your stories
your every everlasting song
is where my heart and soul belong
Your everlasting songs echoes
in the realm of eternity
I keep them near close to my heart
for forever and forever.


**~Majda Ulfat**

# Whisper from You

Every time I kneel to pray
I wish you to be happy
Everyday!

When you left I felt so blue
Tears didn't stop
Falling down too

My legs were numb
I couldn't move on
I want your strength
For the life to go on

I want a whisper from you
So much
"Stop crying girl I'm back"

~ M. M. Kavindi Chathurya
Munasinghe

# PAIN IS PAIN

I ask myself everyday
Was knowing everything enough?

Would I have been able to
Relieve your pain.
Was that really enough?

I was miles away from you,
But could I ever change your
Dull pain into elation?


~ Agamya Sharma

# Love

In the end what makes us continue is "love"
the love we couldn't give and the love we
gave
under the long rains of uncertainty
all the emotions gather under umbrella of
love.
all the emotions become love.
I may not be by your side
but I am always on your side.


~ Majda Ulfat

# Twinkling Eyes

I didn't fall in love
With the best of you
The way you laugh and smile
With twinkling eyes
Make me happy
The way your personality stands out
And the way you dance
Feel me excited
The way your voice touches my soul
I'm having butterflies flutter in my heart
I fell in love with an amazing soul

I want to see and hear you more
But I envy the angels
Who's with you in heaven
Even more

**~ M. M. Kavindi Chathurya
Munasinghe**

# YOUR COMFORT

You brought me warmth,
When I was cold.
You brought me smile,
When all I did was cry.
You brought me laughter,
When I only felt pain.
Yes, you were that comfort to me,
When I was all alone.


~ Suhani Hanotwal

# Lifetime

I wonder if this lifetime is enough
to give you all the love I want
I wonder if this lifetime is enough
to give thanks to the God for your existence
And every time you smile
I come to know that
this lifetime is not enough.


~ Majda Ulfat

# Incomplete

This heart is heavy,
Like a cloud filled with rain,
These tears are contained in me.

So won't you come hold me,
Fix my heart which is incomplete,
Won't you turn back when I call,
Your name my only remedy.

Because when I see you,
I see a sunshine,
Filled with a bright light,
Day like in heaven.

Set me free from this darkness,
Get my scars to heal,
Because without you,
I am incomplete...!

~ Jasia Samreen

# Blue Night Radio

To the Blue Night Radio's storyteller
Will you listen to me?
Will my words ever reach you?


Sometimes, I feel like a fool.. for writing in
second person
But my heart can't help it. I need this void
and so do many..
This is ours to keep..


All I know is, when once in a blue moon on
a blue night
I turn my radio on ..you come back to me.


Radio, such a beautiful way to connect and
give solace to people..
now disappearing.
When you hosted Blue Night Radio show,
from February 2, 2014 to April 2, 2017
It gave people like me hope

To listen to strangers and still somehow
feel familiar.
Everytime, as I turn on the Blue Night
Radio
I hear you.. and your words mending souls,
all over the world.
Even though, your own soul was hurt.


When you said, "I looked at the moon
tonight and it was so pretty" ..I did not feel
alone
anymore.


When you said, "I think it's ok to feel lost in
your life" ..I felt ok, to not be ok.
When you said, "It's alright to gain strength
even tomorrow" ..it gave me hope.


You said, "when your tears are falling,
just let them shed" ..so let my tears shed,
everytime I
listen to you, I think you'd say it's ok.

When you said, "the most beautiful thing
in all the world is right now.
This moment. You.
Don't ever forget that" ..I could love myself
again.


Jonghyun, "my heart is sincere right now.
We'll see eachother again."
Saranghaeyo.. always.


# ~ Mohima Sarkar

# Under the Moonlight

Darkness surrounded me
Once in a gloomy-blue night
Devouring my heart viciously
Leaving the soul with no light
Drowning in that icy ocean
Having no more strength to fight
Waiting for the end desperately
Still vanishing from the sight

An illumination gleamed suddenly
Right from the Moonlight
Followed by 4 mellow rays
Spreading comfort, warmth & light
Granting the place with hope & glee
Colouring my sky blue & white

SHINing glints fell the air pleasingly
Making it more than bright
Bringing happiness & peace
Filling life with serenity & delight

May Lord bless these heavenly souls
& protect them of any plight
Grant them every wish they want
Lead us & them to the path of right.


# ~ Najia Essa Kashcool

# He is the one

Someone asked me
who is that person
on your phone's lock screen
on your closet's door ?
I smiled and replied
I can't possibly define it in few words
but let me try to summarise it for you
He is the one
Who is my umbrella in the rain
my light in dark
my hope in despair
he is all the warmth that I need to live
through the winter
my inspiration to continue my compass
when I feel lost my space
when world shakes me up my voice
when I cant speak my poet
my poetry, my reason
when everything loses meaning
a star that guides me in dark
the brightest star on my sky....

**~ Majda Ulfat**

# The comforting star

The star above in the sky, I thank you for
providing me with comfort in my gloomy
nights.
Your luminosity lights up my whole universe
and drive the darkness out of my life.

When I look at you with my dejected eyes,
you flicker and tell me the secret remedy to
my maladies.
Quotidian I wait for the tiresome day to
pass by and comes the night bringing you to
me.

Seeing you play and dance up in the sky
cures my maladies than any of the folk
suggested antidotes.
Without a fail, I go searching for you every
night
Seeing you distant and faraway causes
sorrow to my heart but it equally brings me

comfort and warmth no one else can
bestow.
Therefore every night I sit under the sky
thanking you for being there, just like you
always were.


~ Noora Baloch

# See you Again

They say world is full of colours
yet I find myself again
staring in the space
searching for your trace
drawing your face
in clouds
You are far away
but I am here at same place
same time
Your memories are my assets
your smile is my strength
your voice is the song of my heart
I know we will meet again
then there will be no pain
I know our goodbye is promised hello
I'll see you again oh, dearest fellow
I'll hear your voice sweet and mellow
You are my brightest star
you are my guide
you are my pride.

**~ Majda Ulfat**

# ASCENDING ANGEL

Close your eyes & ease your heart,
The angels are here to see you off.
To break you away from the burdens of life,
The endless chain of pain! you were in
hostile.
Here and now every hardship and wrestle
has been defied.
Hence, leave sorrow with all your worries
behind.
Now only with angels, stars and flowers you
are intertwined.
Close your eyes & ease your heart,
The angels are here to see you off.


~ **Noora Baloch**

# He went unnoticed

On the spotlight,
he shines bright.


On stage,
a voice so mellow,
even with age,
You put your all for your solo.


Your eyes filled with tears,
we failed to see your fears.


We watched you thanked us,
with your words of trust,
we just couldn't adjust.


Your footsteps grew faint,
your shadow danced,
our shrieks of cries made it paint,
wishing it wasn't a trance.


~ **Sofea**

# Breathe Under the Moon

I remember having many tears when you
were gone
The last day, getting news about you
suddenly breaking my heart
Like a complete bracelet breaks into many
pieces of beads
The pain slowly take control of me
Sometimes feel like out of my breathe
But if I keep that feeling, you will be sad,
right?
So I try to endure the intense of missing you
until night
Only to find you
Just for relief my heart
Cuz I just can breathe under the Moon,
You,
JongHyun


**~ Ratna Haryati**

# I will continue

Same time ticking on the clock
no matter how they mock
I am still in shock
It feels like my optimism hitting the bottom
rock
I am gathering all my hopes to knock
at the door of miracle
to you, it may sound lyrical
but for me even breathing is obstacle
because I miss you
Out of longing and love I have for you
With the little flickering spark
I have, I will continue to walk
through the dark
I will continue to smile
through every trial.


**~ Majda Ulfat**

# Hope

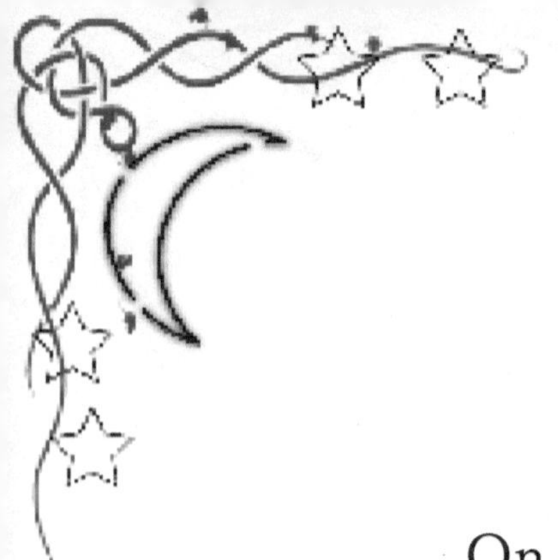

On every blue night,
My heart reminisce.


An angel ascended to heaven,
To make the skies more bright.


Still shining in the stars,
To turn the sorrows in surprise.


Spreading ever lasting love,
And a path filled with light.


Not just saving souls,
But bringing hope to their lives!


~ Jasia Samreen

# LEGEND

He was
A great son, to his parents.
A loving brother, to his sister.
A cheerful father, to his dog.
A loyal member, to his bandmates.
A kind soulmate, to his lover.
And an unforgettable artist, to his fans.


**~ Suhani Hanotwal**

# Reflection

I sat at the side of the lake
Feeling night atmosphere
Cold wind and the shining of the moon from
the sun
I realized something after my eyes catch up
the reflection in the lake
The moon reflection
So bright
So beautiful
Remind me of you
I will never feel lonely again
Cuz I believe you are always with me
From the sky
You look at me brightly, right?
Still gives me the strength to live in a
day
Until night falls,
Until I meet you again

## ~ Ratna Haryati

# I Remember you

I remember you – When the flowers bloom
I remember you – When the birds sing
I remember you – When the tree branches
dance in the wind
I remember you – When the rain fall
I remember you – When the rainbow shines
I remember you – When the sun and moon
rise on day and night
I remember you – When the stars glow at
the night sky

But most of all I remember
Each day and from the start
You will be forever in my heart


**~ M. M. Kavindi Chathurya
Munasinghe**

# "ALWAYS WITH YOU"

Day passes ,passes months
Passing years···
But the pain still remains same
As if time had stopped
Those moments of your still
Remains in my solitude heart

Let anyone say anything
Let no one see your tough times
We are ALWAYS WITH YOU
We are still gonna be with you
Even from the other dimension of world
Somewhere from distance
We SUPPORT you
Sorry, for noticing yours feelings late ,
We were late···
We were a bit too late
Now , regression stays in
Corner of our heart

Still getting the lingering
Pain feeling inside our hearts
Now time is passing ,

Days are going
The months going
Gonna pass the whole year
But still our hearts
Carrying the love for you will never change
Always will have a warm place in our heart for
you
**"YOU DID WELL"**


**~ Samprikta Das**

# Sanctuary

A single thought of you
cleanses my tainted heart,
washes away all my doubts
and vanishes every regret
Your thought is my resting place,
my haven, at the end of tiring day
It's a place of reassurance for
my uncertain self
Your thought is nothing less
than a sanctuary for me.


~ **Majda Ulfat**

# You are priceless

You told me to hold this. But you have no idea
that how can i do
that.
The pain is still same...
I still don't want to accept that you are gone;
Can you come again???
I know that is not possible. Baby you know?
My tears always remind me that how much I
Love and miss
you.
I had only one dream to see you in real..
At least once..
And You are a bad boy...You didn't gave me a
chance....


You can be divine..
You're like a Blue moon - which comes at once.
You're like a single drop of water - which fallen
to the desert..

You shine bright like a diamond - which is
expensive.

You're like a drug and no rehab can fix it....
My heart is beating so fast.. And i don't know
how to turn that
feeling into words..
This is just a momentary goodbye...
I'll be waiting for you.
Let's meet again...
You did well, Kim JongHyun.


~ **Shainy Prarthana**

# Even dream is suffice

Tonight when I close my eyes
and search for you
on the night sky
just descend from the moon
and let me hear your voice
How nice
it would feel to hear your voice
it would be a gift a pure rejoice
like a rose in winter
like a spring in crusty ice
For me, even to dream
is more than suffice.


~ **Majda Ulfat**

# A Diamond

A diamond to remind you
Even we are apart
Your cheerful spirit will
Be in my heart
Forever and more


~ M. M. Kavindi Chathurya
Munasinghe

# Until we meet again

Goodbye are not forever,
Goodbye is not the end,
For every day I miss you,
For every minute I feel you,
For every second I want you,
It simply means I miss you.
Goodbye for now,
Until we meet again.
Goodbye my Love


**~ Shainy Prarthana**

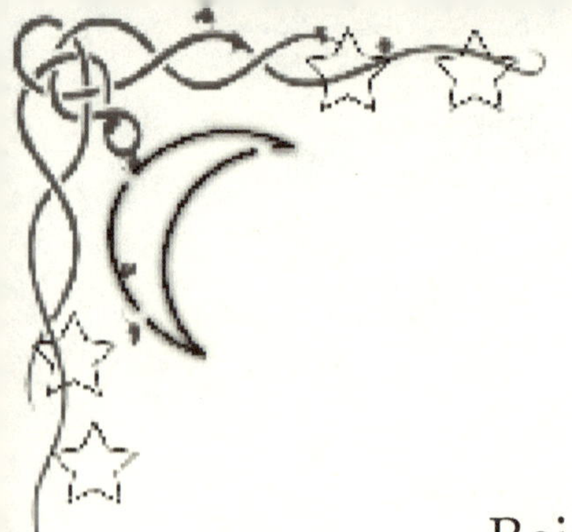

# Poet

Being idol is not easy
But you're idol
So it's really great for you
I remember when I was interested in you
When Ballad unit came up with gorgeous vocal
Also you, the stunning one
Your voice is healing
Unique and getting so emotional
And then you came up with another stunning
arts
By music, lyric ,melody and all
You are..
One of Poet that be a meaningful human
charger


~ Ratna Haryati

# Never gone

You will never be gone
You will never be forgotten
Forgotten are those who are gone
You live in the songs you sang
In the words of the poems you left behind
You are alive in the places you have been
In all of the people's lives you have saved
You will always be preserved in those things
And remain evergreen and forevermore
alive in us.


**~ Noora Baloch**

# Our space

I feel like a nomad
lost in thoughts
trapped between what I am
and what I am supposed to be
searching for the paths
that don't really exist
with my soul wandering
from place to place
I am a nomad
having nowhere to go
yet having every where to go
I might get tired from time to time
I might fall down and cry
or give up for a time
when tired from whole world
and nowhere to go
when hope happiness begin to fade
when little light in my life
starts to flicker and about to go out

your warm words keeps me going
because the space you created
extends infinitely
where I find my solace
your space


No, our space keeps me going
when lost in the haze,
while trapped in a maze
then it no longer matter
who I am
where I am
wherever I am
thanks to our space
I am home...


~ Majda Ulfat

# Can we have another chance ?

I'm speechless.
It hurts me all the time.
No one can criticise you when you are silent.
But only You know that what you did was right.
We all know It was a quick decision.

I don't know whether I can see you again.
I wish you to reborn again among us.
Sometimes when we travel unexpected
happen.
Maybe for the better or unfortunately.

I know that you were never happy from your
heart.
But you pretended that you are okay and you
are happy.
We never understand how you felt.
You have no idea that how much we love you.

You are my Inspiration.
You protected me from all kinds of problems.

But we failed to protect you.
I really want to tell you how much i love you.
But I have no enough words to describe it.
I never want to say goodbye to you.
Because I know that the Moon will never leave
the sky..
You are my Shooting Star.

Thank you so much for coming into my life.
No matter where were you. Stay happy and
peacefully.
That's the the only thing I need.
I will pray everyday as you said.
Because I won't hurt⋯
But can we have another chance to meet?
Then meet me, out of this cruel world.
In a world where there is no pain,
But only love.

**~ Shainy Prarthana**

# Blue Moon

That reminiscent setup,
a voice more notable.

The three decades we've listened,
your wise, comforting words.

One tried conveying a message,
though looks deceived notions,
none grasp his true intentions.

before long,
he departed.

We're disarrayed,
his light dimmed,
vanished into thin air.
Our emotions soared as we mourned,
the numbness and grievance we yearned.
through dusk and dawn,
but now, he is gone.

~ **Sofea**

# Together

We are astrological sign
Connected to each other
Make pattern ,beautifully
We are like that
Even you not here ,we never be separated
You still shine bright decorate our pattern
You still there
Shinning side by side with us
Remember it


~ **Ratna Haryati**

# Agit (아지트)

I often find my days beginning
with endless wandering
and ending with empty sigh
but your voice your words
your laughter, your smile
your memories, your stories
are a precious treasure
a pure pleasure
They beckon me to face every storm
in every cold, they keep me warm
They are a place of refuge, a hide-out
( agit)
to my tired self where I can rest
at the end of tiring day.
Thank you for this "agit"
which remains intact and ever extending for
us.
It is no less than a luxury for us.

~ **Majda Ulfat**

# UNTIL YOU

I hide my feelings,
Knowing that it hurts.
I hide my tears,
Knowing that the time that's gone, will
never come back.
I hide my love,
Knowing that I cannot love again.
When you left me,
A big part of me left with you.
But, let us not cry because you're gone,
Instead, let us be happy that you were here.
Let's be happy that we cherished each and
every moment of that we
were together.
Let us not forget that we all went went
through a lot. TOGETHER.

So today, I wanna take this opportunity to
tell you that

Kim JongHyun, I miss you very much, my love.

It's been 3 years and our memories are lively.
I wanna tell you that, you were the bravest one out there.
I wanna tell you that I love you so much
And that I'll never ever forget you.
Even if I intend to forget all my memories,
But our memories together will still live.
Maybe that you were here,
I was able to know the meaning of Love,
Cherish, Joy,
And what not.

Thank you so much JongHyun for giving me my world.
I love you so much, my dear.
I'll always remember us this way.
You did well honey... You did well.

**~ Suhani Hanotwal**

# Poetry

I have definitely read you before
yet every time I get new and different
meaning
From heart to soul
you are a poetry
world is full of fancy words
but they are just alphabets clumped
together
as mere words ,simple sentences
so predictable and plain
they are nothing compared to you
You are a poetry
we don't need rhymes and meters
you are so harmonious as it is
no metaphor no simile can personify you
You are a sijo, tanka, haiku
sonnet, ballad, free verse, limerick,
all in one

I am reading you
then I trying to interpret you
you've left Keats, Shelley ,Byron in awe
such a beautiful poetry you are
poetry, I can't comprehend
poetry, that I can't forget
poetry that has transcended time
poetry ,that has me
all mesmerized
all hypnotised
all the so called beautiful words are
shallow and empty in front of you
they hold no meaning to me
not blinded,
not obsessed,
not possessed,
I'm enlightened by this heavenly poetry
poetry called you.


~ **Majda Ulfat**

# OUR MEMORIES

This is what I'm gonna tell my kids.
Before I met your father,
I met him.
Before I loved your father,
I loved him.
Maybe for him, I was just a girl in the
crowd,
But for me, he was more than my world.


Never thought we would part our ways,
Without reaching to our ends.
But then I realised,
We were living in a parallel universe,
And that, he already reached his end.
Without telling anyone,
He came and went,
And made such a beautiful impact on our
lives.
Living without him was like,
A human living without oxygen.

But then, I was happy.
Happy to know he existed
And we shared a lot of memories together.
Happy to know that he was my first love.
Whenever I cried, my tears were happy
tears.
Because I knew, he went through a lot.
And he was the courageous one, fighting all
alone.

I do not regret a thing,
Because regretting only makes our world
sorrow.
Instead, I cherished things,
Because I knew, cherishing things would
lead to a whole new world.
A world where our merry memories still
live.

So dear, fill your heart not with sorrow,
But with love.
Because all of us know that he's always
there for us.

Maybe, we might feel his physical absence,
But knowing that he's living in our hearts,
Never let us feel empty.
And that's where I call my story
OUR MEMORIES.


~ Suhani Hanotwal

# My Shooting Star

After from now.
I'll breathe only for your name.
Do you know that??
When you feel the warmth of my heart and
that's enough.
Please come back to me.

If you come back,
I want to be with you.
When the day I gave up on my last breath,
That tells how much you mean to me.

I felt the way that you are mine.
Smile on your face, can make me dizzy.
And your angelic voice can make me
comfortable.
I know that you are singing for me from the
sky.
Can I come to you to stay with you all the time.

No matter how I felt..
I'm always happy because you are in my heart.
My life has found it's missing piece.
Can you hear me?
Are you listening to me?
You are my shooting Star.
Please come back again soon.
I'll be waiting...


~ Shainy Prarthana

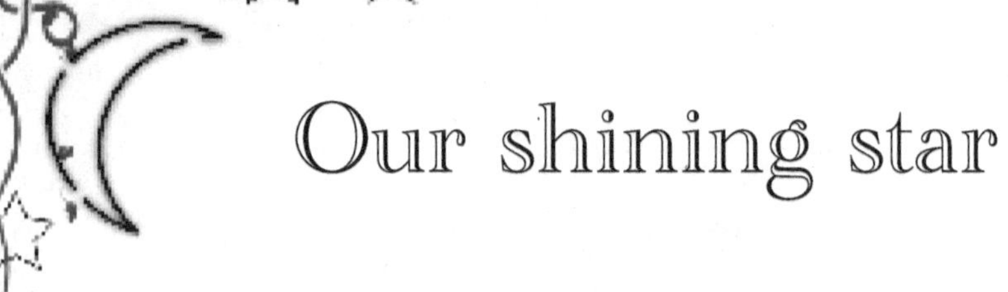

# Our shining star

Flecks of gold,
Stopped in time,
Reflects a soul,
With beauty, divine.

Even his mortal form is as beautiful,
Those kind and caring eyes,
With a heart made of gold.

A person, a gift or a blessing,
His words are like sorrows,
And like the blooming spring.

A star shining among a million lights,
The highest in the sky,
And the brightest at night...!

**~ Jasia Samreen**

# Small Bundles of Joy

Looking at your dreamy eyes,
Hearing your joyous laugh,
Listening to your melodious voice,
Seeing your bright smile,
And, you.


**~ Noora Baloch**

# Writing Your Story

My heart is weary
but I won't call you a mere memory
through the times I will carry you in my
heart,
oh my brightening sanctuary
I will continue to write your story
to show everyone your light your glory


~ **Majda Ulfat**

# I Miss You

When I feel out of my limit
I remember you
you give me some strength through Breathe
when I feel like people around ignoring me
You give me praise through End of the Day
when I feel like no place to scratch my pencil
You make me believe I can share my thoughts
with other through Elevator,
like I have many paper to write my diary
I might look okay
Still can remembering your beautiful poems
through many good song
but sorry
I miss you


~ Ratna Haryati

# NEVER ENDING

Even if one day
The sun never rises,
And the moon never sets.
My love for you will never rest.

# YOU

A million stars in the sky,
Only one shining bright.
And that's you.


~ Suhani Hanotwal

# Aqua Pearl

You coloured the Moon
Coloured the stars
You coloured the
Ocean with the sky

You coloured the
Light sticks
Coloured the Stage
You coloured
Korea and coloured
The World

You Coloured Shawols
With one Colour;
Aqua Pearl

~ **M. M. Kavindi Chathurya
Munasinghe**

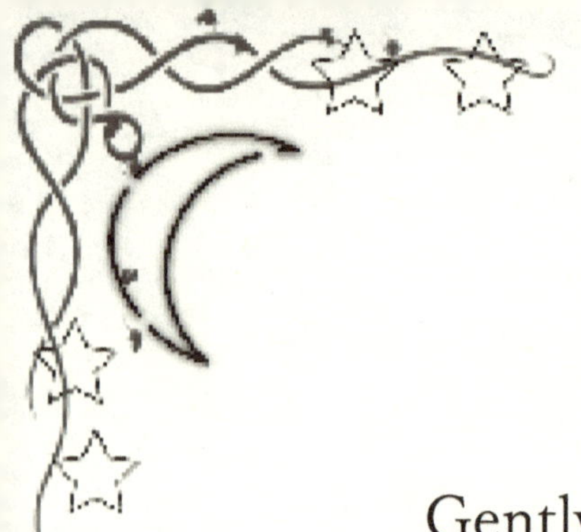

# Angel

Gently spread your wings
wrap them around me as rings
unravel all the confusing strings
save me from staggering swings

I have always been wrong
you always stood strong
without you each moment is so long
I have nowhere to belong

Save me from every liar
take me out of this mire
take me higher
ignite my heart with passionate fire

With your warmth pat my shoulder
on my own its getting colder
don't let me surrender
protect me from coming boulder

So strangulating is my tear
so suffocating is my fear
please tell me you are here
tell me you are near


My words are to read
my voice is to heed
no matter how far paths may lead
you are the only one I need.


**~ Majda Ulfat**

# HOLDING US TIGHT

You were looking for support,
So I gave you my hand.
You grabbed it tightly,
And walked this journey with me.
At a point, our grip loosened,
And with you,
You took all these scars and fears.
Leaving me with only memories..

# NORTH STAR

In my journey of love and hate,
You were like a North Star.
Shining brightest in the dark sky,
And finally showing me my path.

**~ Suhani Hanotwal**

# A parallel universe story

Somewhere in the parallel universe,
I hope you got through this,
You and I, we survived this together.

You are giving us many more music,
You and your music grew more there
We recently celebrated out 12th anniversary
together
Thank god! It was during your vacation.

You gifted us with most beautiful ballads,
Maybe Story Of Op 3.

We were overwhelmed by your words in Fifth
Solo concert
You said tears are also a way of speaking
As you whipped towards the Pearl Aqua Ocean
Making us go speechless.
Our story keeps getting bigger, So is our
fandom.

You are falling in love with Roo more and
more,
Just like little SHINee dates, Roo, Commedes,
Garcons, Adam and Eve are enjoying their
dates too,
You again hacked SMEnt. to upload Roo
atrocity.


Amma and Sodam Unnie surprises you with
their visits
You received gifts for yours 30th birthday from
all over the world
To the point where even ROK was shocked.
Did you feel us even when you were serving
military ?


Minho still annoys you with his height,
You still surprise k-shawols with those little
visit to their work places
And do you know I-shawols are still feeling
jealous about that.


We promised we'll overwhelm each other with
love

We are going stronger and Bigger than ever.
Some best bonds are only felt.
SHINee x Shawols

81


~ Yuva Karnika

# Halo

There is a person
who warmed my world with his smile
and shone like a sun like a moon
to me he is like the star
brighter than Sirius
and a guiding star
like Polaris
But to much of my dismay
that star had set earlier
I was afraid
I would be lost in darkness
I was afraid how would live
it all felt meaningless
but I have realized
beautiful humans are like stars
whose warmth and light can be felt
from beyond the horizon
humans are like too

their warmth and light
can be remembered and felt

while being on other side
their memories are like
halo of a star that can surpass
the limit of horizon
those memories can shine beyond
the boundaries of this world
and time and space
undoubtedly his precious moments
and memories continue to shine on us
and show us our way when lost in dark.


~ Majda Ulfat

# You are my Inspiration

When the Nights are covered by thick
darkness,
You are the Moon which Brights up my World.
When the painting fade from the water drops,
You are the Sun that Shone to prevent it.
The moment I fell out of the line,
You were the one.
Who gave me the Strength to Stand upright.
At a time, when the life itself was boring,
You were An encouragement to me.
Do I live Today?
That's because of you..

You showed me the reality of our Life.
You taught me the best lesson.
Which is that 'Death is not a Solution to all
your Problems'.
And I thank you enough for that.
You gave me the pain of losing loved once.

Thank you so much for what you did for me,
for us.
I will be loving you till my last breath.
I love you and miss you.
You did well, Our prince, You did well..


# ~ Shainy Prarthana

## 200813
## -A letter wrote on the 1000th day without you-

I loved you today, like every other days
I missed you today, like every other days
You are the only eternal person I'd long for
I gain more strength and comfort talking to
you
You are our blessing
Now I realize what it truly means when they
say
"Even death can't separate us"
May we meet again,
In another Good day,
In another Good life.
Love you--


~ Yuva Karnika

# Long Enough As Eternity

I don't know much about distances
physical distances don't matter
Farther you go
closer you are
to my heart
I feel you
in the rhythm of my heart beat
I see you
through my soul
your presence lingers
strongly behind my smiles
that voice of yours and that laughter
resonates within my ears
your fainting traces
have solid tracks
you are here
in the depths of my eyes
just tell me how much lasting
is this thing they say
to the moon and back
is it long enough to be called
as eternity ?

**~ Majda Ulfat**

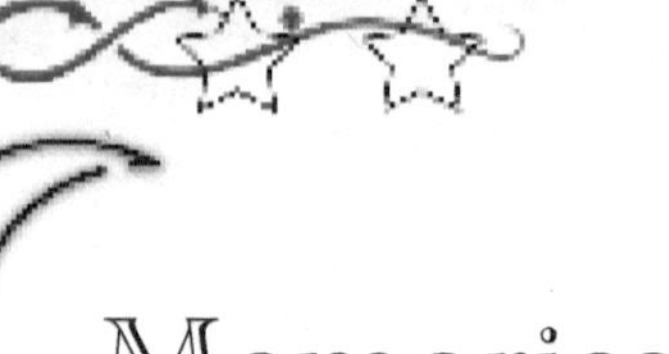

# Memories that speaks us

I took out a piece of paper and a pen to
write a poem in your praise.
With the bursting memories of yours my
emotions spread all over the place.

The tears started rushing down my cheeks
and soaked the entire page.
I tried to control my overwhelming self and
finally began to write.
I wrote a sentence or two and gave myself
some time to think.

I pondered why it is harder than it seems,
my mind is a garden filled with memories
of yours so why is it so hard to pen them
down?
I wrote pages after pages and tore them into
pieces one after another.

I wondered out loud, is it because I know
my words would never do justice to the
person you are.


No words in the world could describe the
beauty of your soul and the giving person
you always have been.
Then why I still take out yet another piece
of paper to write a page just to tear it down
again ?



~ Noora Baloch

# SHINE

You radiate brightness, Smiles,
And Moonlight.


## Our Fairy Boy


Perhaps the fairies up there,
Saw how beautiful you were,
So they decided to make you theirs.


**~ Yuva Karnika**

# WISH YOU WERE HERE

In the midnight glimmer,
I sat so idle on a swing.
And when the lights go dimmer,
I think of the beauty of a wing.

What angelic powers you've got,
You seem to allure me so well.
I miss your heavenly smile,
That faded away in the cold spell.

I think of you every night,
And all the memories that seemed so bright.
I never knew that you were in pain,
Because you always looked so blissful and
fain···

~ Agamya Sharma

# Who knows ?

We say you left prematurely,
But you know that day was your chosen day.
we created a thousand reasons,
Only you know the right reason..
we say we should have been patient,
Only you know how patient you were.
A beautiful, talented person is a rarity to us,
You are the man who has never seen a rare
man.

We think that love is common to you,
But only you know who you really want.
We think you should have told someone,
But only you know if who should have asked.
You think we should have saved you,
You know that there was no one who didn't
think so.
We think you are not strong,
You know the times you endured more than
that.

This was not enough for people to blame you,
But we know that you were the most in pain
and you endured
it well. You did well love, you've been through
a lot.
Rest well now.


~ Shainy Prarthana

# SOLACE

The tears that you've shed
Are now forgotten
And now only a genuine smile paints your
face
As you use the wings that you've gained
To ascend to a better place
And that day
All the teardrops that've fallen from your
angel eyes
Dissipated into the sky,
They stained the moon blue
In hopes that the now hued moon
Would bring comfort to the people crying
for you···

**~ Syna Kaur Anand**

# You are here

Now that I am making memories
with your memories stories,
with your words
therefore for me you are here
only my eyes can't see that you are here
but my heart knows so there's nothing to
fear
there fore I won't shed any tear.
l can see you with my closed eyes
my anxious heart still calms down only to
your lullabies
I have felt you without any physical form
thanks to you in the frost I still feel warm
I try to be not sappy
I just pray you are happy
we are in a place far from words of longing
so rather than shouting out I miss you to the
sky
I just whisper I love you to the wind
with the belief this wind can blow to the
heavens.

**~ Majda Ulfat**

# Not just

Do you know?
The seeds can grow and blooms
Even it has flowers or no
Seeds through many path to survive and reach
their peak of development
Through the hard and soft phase,
Seeds not called as seed anymore after that
They are plant ,adult plant
It's like you
You not just idol who follow the flow
You're Jonghyun
You gave a lot of many effort making beautiful
melody through music
The strong seed that I know
It's like you
You are not just music or melody
You're Jonghyun
The special one
Gave many people happiness like beautiful

seeds who grow as plant

## ~ Ratna Haryati

# TEAR IN MY EYE

Thoughts of you drift into my mind
As I stare out the window
I let the thoughts of you consume me
As I look out the twinkling stars,
Repeating, "You Did Well"
While a tear in my eye slides past.
As I talk about you
I try to smile through the pain,
But I miserably fail
Because there's a tear in my eye
That's just waiting to fall down
That tear in my eye, is rolling through my
cheeks now
I wonder if you're seeing us
But the one thing I know,
If you're looking from up above
I know that you'll be smiling at us···


**~ Syna Kaur Anand**

# Shining From Afar

I find myself staring in the space
searching for your trace
drawing your face
and in that finding my solace
Your word's your voice's warm embrace
Melt all the sorrowful glace
I'll adorn your memories with poem
until we meet again
I'll survive every storm
and all the rain
Neither would I try to escape
not would I shed your memories as tears
instead all wear them as cape
fighting all the demons all the fears
You are
Helping me fight every lament every scar
Guiding me like a brightest star
Shining from afar

**~ Majda Ulfat**

# Mr. Moon

It's at the
" END Of THE DAY "
When the moon is
" SHININ"
Feeling all " LONELY"
I sit at the window
Taking a deep " BREATH"
Looking at the
" MOON"
Because he is my
" OBSESSION"
He is my
" INSIPIRATION"
I tell him, you are
" BEAUTIFUL TONIGHT"
he replied
" LIKE YOU"
He started saying
"LOVE IS SO NICE"
and even " CRAZY"

Ending it with
the lines I am the
" ONLY ONE YOU NEED "
"ONLY THE WORDS, I LOVE YOU"
and hides behind the clouds
and as i close my eyes
with my head rested on
the window panes
the words
" ALWAYS BE WITH YOU"
Shine bright within my heart.


~ P. Deekshitha

# SO GOODBYE

It always seems to amaze me,
How quickly change occurs.
Like a constant flowing river,
Near an icy cold waters.
Like the tides change,
Bringing newness.
Like the wind blows,
In the fresh air.
I know things never stay the same,
But this time, it's just not fair.

I feel like, I just met you and now you move
away.
And I smile, knowing that, this is your last
day.
I pray we'll keep in touch,
I pray because the past I'd say those things
and try it,
But those things don't seem to last.

You're the love that I've met,
I cherished you a bunch.

And although our time is been short,
Know, I love you very much.
I will always be here for you,
To talk, to listen, to write,
At the very least in spirit,
If I am not in a clear plain sight.
Email, write or call me,
I'll always lend an ear.
My schedule is not so crazy,
You know, I'm always here.

I know, one day I'll visit you and
You'll be back I'm sure.
All I hope is that our love lasts,
The test of time, so pure.
All I end this thought, I know there's more,
So much more there is to say.
But I'll leave that for another time,
Another lovely day.

## ~ Suhani Hanotwal

# Letters
# to
# Jonghyun

18.12.2017

Dear JongHyun,

How are you doing ? Are you okay ? Are you happy ? Are you tired ? Are you resting well ?

I have a lot of things to ask. But as soon as I try to pen them down, every word flows down in the form of tears from my eyes.

I was numb. I was unconscious. All the memories flashed, playing from the first day you introduced yourself as SHINee's JongHyun till I saw you in your last concert.

Then I remembered all you said to us. All your teachings. All your hard works. And what not···

I still not complaint because I know you went through a lot.

Maybe we were not aware of what you were bearing. But we still couldn't forgive ourselves.

Leaving all of us behind, yet loving us and singing for us from the night sky is really everything to us.

All I wanna say is that,
You did well, honey.
You really went through a lot.
And yes, I couldn't keep my promise to not cry every night, writing to you.
I love you very much, JongHyun.
Please be safe and happy and hear to all of us, especially our SHINee everyday. We all miss you very much.

With Love

~ **Suhani Hanotwal**

18.12.2020

Today was something else,
because he was something else.
I spent the whole day cherishing his work
and remembering him for who he was.
He was a larger than life person.. and I've
come to realise.. that for people like him, this
world is not enough.
Your last words to your sister were,
"It was really hard up till now.
Send me off please.
Tell me I did well.
This is my last greeting"

YOU DID WELL, JongHyun.. more than
words can say..

We all will unite again, we will all be together..
your four diamonds and your blue ocean
Will meet you on a blue night, under a blue
moon.
Till then, be happy wherever you are Oppa.
Saranghae!
~ **Mohima Sarkar**

18.12.2020
Dear JongHyun,

Like any other year religiously I sit to write you a letter that cannot be delivered to you anymore. Helplessly I write yet again, praying my words became a song and reaches to you up in the heavens above.

It's been three years already! I can't believe it. Time flies. It feels like yesterday. I thought with time I will forget, I thought with time the wound would heal itself as if time is the ointment for my scars of that day. However, I was wrong I was gravely wrong. Time or any other thing would never be able to ease the pain of how you left this world. It would never ever lessen the heartbreak I felt for you. I will never look at the world same again because you not being here changed everything in my life.

I'm so sorry that you have to go through all that pain. You did so well, you went through a lot, and I am so proud of you. I say all of that and still wish you were here that you had another chance at life that all of the

things that went the way they, happened differently. Or at least you exist in another dimension jolly, happy and doing all of the things you loved and being the most sweetheart that you were cause you deserved the world. You deserve it more than anyone in this globe.

♡I miss you so much

~**Noora**

25.01.2021

To my dearest husband......

How have you been baby? You know what, Blingers all around the world are going to publishing a book for you.

I know you are so happy and proud of our Family. Here are so many good hearted people who are supporting each others. Those girls are always ready to do anything for you. They all love you very much.

Baby, give Blingers your blessings to fight all the obstacles they face.

I know that you are always here to support us. That thinking can motivate me well. You are the most precious person I've ever met in my life.. Day by day I miss you, I miss your voice, I miss your smile, I miss your cuteness, I miss your baby face, and I miss your everything.. But it's ok... I know that you are in here with Us. Do you have any idea that how much I love you?

Yes.. How much I love my father that much I love you..

I'm so excited to read the complete version of this book.. Every shawol writing this book turned their own feelings into words..that's what you taught us. Right? This can be very expensive and the beautiful book in this world. I am so happy.

I have to go now. We will finish this and publish this soon as we can.. And also one thing; There is a girl named Suhani and you have to keep her on your mind always. Without her we cannot meet our ends.. I really want to thank her. Thank you so much for gave me this much of love and this much of confidence.. I'll write you soon again..

You Did Well JongHyun. I love you....

~Shainy

- Shany -
21 - 01 - 26

26.01.2021
Dear JongHyun Oppa,

Oppa, I'm shawol Kavindi, from Sri Lanka. I am a huge fan of SHINee five since 2008. And specially a fan fallen in with your angelic voice.

You told that, you debut to support your family, because they were the reason and the joy which was your driven force of doing music. That proves how much you loved your family, you always supported and cheered your SHINee brothers when you always had a chance, that proves how much you cared for your team mates. You raised Roo very dearly and Roo is the luckiest dog in the wold. You always smiled and thanked honestly to the Shawols who supported you and cheered you.

That proves how much you loved the people around you. Your voice and quotes from blue night always made my heart at ease and filled with joy.

The funny moments of gags you did on stage and in TV programmes made me laugh every time.

From all the singers in K-pop world you are the most talented person I ever knew. As a song writer, author, Blue Night radio host, record producer, entertainer as well as a singer. You showed the musical world a new dimension. And uplifted the K-pop world with your talents.

Even though you left us, I know you're always looking at us with your twinkling eyes from heaven. You said "There is no shortcut to perfection.

All it takes is hard work, and more hard work". And I want to say, you took a long path and succeeded, you did well Jonghyun. I and all the shawols, promise you that we are always loving and remembering you and your great work. You did well Poet| Artist. Love you to the moon and never back.

~ **M. M. Kavindi**

26.01.2021
Dear my Blue moon,

My JongHyun-ah, naya KimJan-ah. How are you doing my man? Hope you're doing good. I wanna say that I am thankful to you. My life was full of worries and filled with sadness, I found your presence in 2013 and I was like Oh my god! his voice and songs are really amazing.

My life continued as it is and my days became harder and harder everyday. Then I started searching for your words the most because it comforted me a lot. Your lyrics are like a mirror of my hardships, the inner meanings made me realise the reality of life. I do have a habit that when I am sad and I want to cry, I won't tell or cry to the people who are in-front of me,I just go somewhere where no one can watch me crying. I cry to you, you to know that.

I have called your name more than the word mom. You were always there for me and I know it but still somewhere in

my heart it aches, that I can't see you in my eyes, whenever I start thinking about the depression you faced I always end up in tears, I just don't want you to be hurt. Also, I can totally feel you my JongHyun-ah, if you have found a person who can feel your pain, you might not have done something that we regret now.

Anyway, I hope that you're happy there. I wish you will be born somewhere in this world again and also have the happy life which you wished to have. You know what? You're my most admirable person. I am thankful to you for entering my life and letting me to love you and keep you in my heart. I miss you so much, my JongHyun-ah. It's really hard for me to move on with my life without you but it's really good to run my life with your beautiful memories.

You gave us plenty and plenty of memories to cherish you, I wanna say this "you saved thousands of people's lives before, now you are saving millions of people's lives by your songs and words" We love you forever.

I keep you in my heart forever my JongHyun-ah. No words can express how much I love you and how much I miss you.

Always in the remembrance of my JongHyun-ah

Your beloved girl


~ **Kimjan**

26.01.2021

Hi

I'm Majda. I've been your fan no, like you said we fans, are your best friend so I'll say you've been my friend since 7 years now.

Thanks to you I experienced unimaginable amount of warmth. You are amazing poet and talented artist and beautiful human and an empath .To me you are always number 1. As a poet myself I always see you as my mentor and my favourite poet I always look up to.

In this world there are endless possibilities, we could've existed in different times and without knowing you but the fact I am able to listen to your voice and see your smile is like a miracle to me. Yes, you are a miracle, rare and precious miracle.

We are always on your side. As fans we have always been receiving so much from you your kind words, your smile, your songs and countless memories. Although we can never possibly reciprocate all the love you gave but

as a tribute and love we have written this book. I hope you would like it. This book and our hearts have one thing in common:
And that's you.

This book and our hearts have endless love and gratitude for you. Thank you for being with us. We love you. We miss you so much.
You did so well.

We are so proud of you.

With Love,

~**Majda Ulfat.**

Dear Jonghyun

I'm Deekshitha, a 19 years old shawol from India. I've been a huge fan of yours ever since I heard your song 'Lucifer' (SHINee). It was in 2015 that i first got to know about you.

Oppa you are a multi-talented person - a singer, song writer, record producer, radio host of Blue Night. And apart from being a great vocalist, you are also a great son and a loving & supportive brother. Your love towards Roo, your pet dog, always makes my heart melt. The first thing that attracted me towards you is your voice, its my favourite sound.

Hearing your voice brings a huge smile on my face making me forget all my pain. I share a special relation with you without ever needing to say how much I'm in love with you. I share all sort of feelings with you, I cry for you and I smile for you. Whenever I feel low, just thinking about you makes me happy and all my pain vanishes.

Your songs, which are more like a therapy to me, helps me to overcome all my tough times. I was like a closed book with nothing written in it, until I got to know you. Jonghyun oppa, you bought a huge change in my life, giving it a meaning and purpose. Every time I miss you, I just look at the moon and smile hoping you are doing well up there.

I could write a hole book for you expressing my feelings towards you, but let me just end it here for now saying I LOVE YOU MY MR. MOON. I will keep loving and supporting SHINee forever.

With love

~ P. Deekshitha

When you're tired and having a hard time
Please let me stay by your side
So I can give back the love I had only received
Before this life ends.
~ SHINee ONEW

To Choose our own way is not an easy thing to do,
But everybody has their own choice.
~SHINee KEY

You are my flower,
Not because you're prettier than other flowers.
You are my flower,
Not because you are more fragrant than other flowers.
You are my flower'
Because you have already blossomed in my heart.
**~SHINee MINHO**

When something's hard, smiling helps us in
the end and it becomes fun.
~SHINee TAEMIN

A formula that will never be broken for a
lifetime,
SHINee + SHINee World = Love.

JongHyun isn't gone.
As long as the sky is blue, and
The sun is still shining,
You will be able to find him.

**Kim Jong-hyun** also known as Jjong, among his fans, was called, Bling Bling Jonghyun. Kim Jonghyun was born on April, 08th 1990, in South Korea. At the age of fifteen, he was discovered by SM Entertainment in 2005, when he played in a song festival with his band mates at school. He dropped out from high school in grade 10 to pursue his dream to become a musician. But later on he attended 'Chungwoon University' before transferring to 'Myongi University', where he received a master's degree in film and musical studies.

***"Even though we cannot communicate using the same language, we use music instead"***
— Kim Jonghyun —

After nearly two and half years of hard training, he debuted as the main vocalist in South Korean boy band with five members, named "**SHINee**" on 25th May 2008 in 'SBS Inkigayo'. He was an innocent, kind hearted, caring member in the band. He always said that,

*"Life is full of chances, take it lightly"*

Since 2009, he contributed to his band as a singer and as a songwriter and on the path of his music career he did a lot of duets and helped composing and writing songs for *SHINee* members as well as for his friends and colleagues. Later on he contributed his talents as a composer in 2013, debuted as a radio host in 2014 in Blue Night radio show MBC, and as a solo singer on 12th January 2015 with his album 'Base'. In September 2015 he published a book which was written about his song writing experience and inspirations, with the title of

*"Skeleton Flower: Things that have been Released and set free"*.

On 24th May 2016 he released his first studio album 'she is' under SM Entertainment. He said that *"one can feel his passion as a singer- song writer the most"* in *"she is"*. On 9th March 2017, MBC confirmed that Jonghyun would leave his position as radio host at MBC Blue Night. He released his second complete album, titled 'Story Op.2' on 24th April 2017. 11th May 2017 Concert, The Agit. And on

9th- 10th December 2017, Jonghyun held Concert titled: Inspired at South Korea Olympic Handball Gymnasium. At the same time, he was working on his new album, which was set to be released in January 2018. Not only to the music industry he also attended various reality shows.

In 2015 he won the **MBC Entertainment award in the category of Excellence award - Radio for Blue Night Radio.**

In 2016 he won the **Golden disk awards in the category of Disk Bongsang for his album Base**. And also nominated for the Mnet Asian Music Award under the category of Best male artist.

In 2019 He won the **Golden disk awards under the category of Disk Bongsang** for his album Poet| Artist and it was also nominated for the disk Daesang and the popularity award. Also won the **Special disk Bongsang** fans choice award. In the same year he won the 13th Annual Soompi Award under the category of Hallyu Special Award.

*"This road I'm walking on is made of my hopes of making my dreams come true and the fragments of passing time. Sometimes, when I look back on my footprints I can see myself dreaming of this present time "*

On 18th December 2017, his sudden death caused a huge shock to the band mates, K-pop world and to the world music industry. However, the album was released posthumously on 23th January 2018, which was named as '**Poet| Artist**'.

**Poet| Artist** debuted at the number 177 on Billboard 2020 with 5,000 equivalent album units, making Jonghyun the forth Korean solo artist to appear on the chart.

*"Life is a series of encounters and farewells. I believe we grow in the process. For now, it's very sad but we will meet again."*

**SHINee was born as 5 and will forever be 5HINee.**
**We miss you, Jonghyun. You will forever be in our hearts. You did well!**